★ ★ ★ ★ ★ *The* ★ ★ ★ ★ ★
CIVIL WAR
KIDS 150

**Fifty Fun Things to Do, See, Make, and Find
for the 150th Anniversary**

CIVIL WAR TRUST

Saving America's Civil War Battlefields
Civilwar.org

Nicole L. Osier, *Editor*
Sheralyn Morehouse, *Editor*
Garry E. Adelman, *Contributing Editor*
Clayton Butler, *Contributing Editor*

LYONS PRESS
Guilford, Connecticut
An imprint of Globe Pequot Press

Lyons Press is an imprint of Globe Pequot Press.

Illustrations by Robert L. Prince

Text design: Sheryl P. Kober
Layout artist: Sue Murray
Project editor: Meredith Dias

Library of Congress Cataloging-in-Publication Data

The Civil War kids 150 : fifty fun things to do, see, make, and find for the 150th anniversary / The Civil
War Trust.
p. cm.
Includes index.
ISBN 978-0-7627-8205-5
1. United States—History—Civil War, 1861–1865—Study and teaching—Activity programs—Juvenile
literature. I. Civil War Trust (U.S.)
E468.C6248 2012
973.7071—dc23
2012004690

Printed in the United States of America

10 9 8 7 6 5 4 3 2 1

CONTENTS

Create

Perform

Find

Read/Watch

When you see this icon, go to the
website for more fun.

INTRODUCTION

History is more than just reading facts and memorizing dates—history is about exploring the past, discovering the unknown, and solving mysteries. This can mean doing things the way they were done in the past, visiting historic places, or finding artifacts.

This book is meant to be a way for *you* to discover the Civil War. We have created fifty fun activities that allow you to experience things on your own.

The activities are divided into four sections: Create, Perform, Find, and Read/Watch. In the Create section you have the opportunity to make something of your own, such as baking hardtack and taking a "then and now" photo. In the Perform section you may sing a Civil War song, hike a battlefield, or model a uniform. In the Find section you'll work as a detective, uncovering mysteries such as where a submarine sank and Franklin Thompson's real name. In the Read/Watch section you will read letters from real soldiers as well as view documentaries and reenactments.

As you complete each activity, check it off on the list. Complete more than thirty and you can count yourself as a Civil War buff. Complete all fifty and you may go on to be the next great Civil War historian!

Special thanks to the National Park Service staff at Stones River National Battlefield and Harpers Ferry National Historical Park for their help with the Signal Flag and the Cause of Death activities. I am grateful to Robert Shenk and his daughter for the awesome cover image. Thanks to Tracey McIntire for her keen eye; to Jeff Rodek for his support with this project; and to Sheralyn Morehouse, Garry Adelman, and Clayton Butler for their hard work, without which this book could not have been completed. Finally, my deepest appreciation to Globe Pequot Press for publishing *The Civil War Kids 150* and seeing the value in a Civil War book especially for kids.

If you liked this book and are thirsty for more, check out *The Civil War 150: An Essential To-Do List for the 150th Anniversary.*

Good luck and have fun!!!

Nicole Osier
Senior Manager, Education Programs
Civil War Trust, Washington, DC

Create

Immerse yourself in the history of the American Civil War through your personal creativity. This is your opportunity to learn about history in ways you may have never imagined.

By completing the activities in this section, you'll actually get to taste the food that soldiers ate, write letters to those who lived during that time, send a "soldier" to battlefields where battles actually took place, and learn how to send coded Civil War messages.

Creating your own materials and projects allows you to discover the past in your own way, without someone telling you exactly what happened.

Have fun with these activities while thinking seriously about how each one relates to the Civil War and what lessons it teaches. If you can, save the projects when you are done and share them with others.

Get creative with the projects; the more you put into them, the more you will get out of them.

Take Your *Flat Civil War Soldier* to the Battlefield

Description: Men were sent off to war leaving many of their loved ones behind. After becoming soldiers, they would spend much of their time training, and would march for days or weeks between battles. Once in battle, soldiers were overwhelmed by the noises, sights, smells, and emotions. Many soldiers gave their lives on battlefields and today we are able to pay our respects by visiting these places.

Directions:

1. Color in the Civil War soldiers on the next page—one is a Union soldier and one is a Confederate soldier.

2. When you visit Civil War sites or complete activities in this book, take a picture of your flat soldier at that place.

3. Also, you can send your soldier to battlefields or other Civil War sites. To do this, write a letter explaining how you are sending your soldier to the battlefield. Include:

   a. Your soldier's name, age, and where he is from.

   b. An explanation to the staff about how you are sending your soldier to Civil War sites.

   c. Ask the staff to take a picture of your soldier at the battlefield.

   d. Have the staff send the picture to kids150@civilwar.org, and the Trust will post the pictures on the Flickr account listed below.

4. All pictures of your flat soldiers can be posted on the Civil War Trust's Flickr account at www.flickr.com/groups/cwkids150.

 www.flickr.com/groups/cwkids150

Confederate

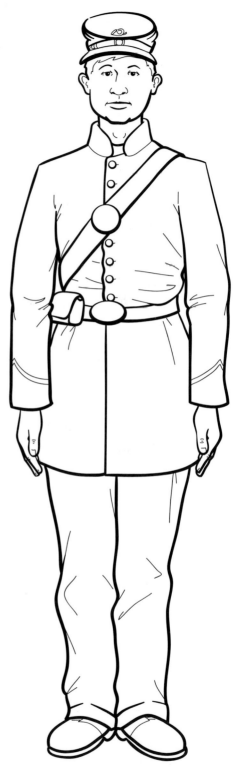

Union

Whip Up a Batch of Hardtack and Have a Try

Description: A Civil War soldier's rations could include the following items: beans, peas, bacon, pickled beef, mixed vegetables, and a cracker-like biscuit called hardtack. Made mostly of flour and water, hardtack was easy to make and easy to store. Hardtack never spoiled; in fact, some museums have hardtack from the Civil War on display! While it would not spoil, however, different types of bugs, including maggots, made their home in hardtack. Named because it's hard as a rock, hardtack generally needed to be soaked in water, coffee, or bacon grease before being eaten.

Make sure to get your parents' permission and help when making your own hardtack.

Army Hardtack Recipe

Yield: 12 hardtack biscuits

2 cups flour   ½–¾ cup water

1 tablespoon shortening   6 pinches salt

1. Preheat oven to 400 degrees.

2. Mix all the ingredients in a medium-size bowl.

3. Knead dough until thoroughly mixed.

4. Spread dough flat on a greased cookie sheet, about an inch thick.

5. Bake for 30 minutes.

6. Remove from oven and cut dough into 3-inch squares. Using a fork, punch four rows of four holes in each square.

7. Turn dough over and return to oven and bake for another 30 minutes.

8. Turn oven off and leave door open.

9. Leave hardtack in oven until cool.

10. The hardtack will keep for 4–5 days.

Make Your Own Signal Flag and Send a Message

Description: With no walkie-talkies or cell phones, how did Civil War soldiers communicate across the vast distances of the battlefield? One way to send messages was through a flag-waving system called "wigwag" signaling. Both the Union and Confederacy instituted a specially trained group called the US Signal Corps. The Signal Corps worked on elevated signal stations during battles, sending messages about troop movement, artillery fire, and other information related to the battle.

Signal flags came in three different colors to use against a variety of backgrounds. The most commonly used flag was white with a red square in the center. Another was red with a white square in the center and was used at sea. A third was black, which could be seen well in snow. Torches were used at night. Messages were sent by waving the flag or torch down to the left and back (**ONE**) or down to the right and up (**TWO**) or a dip in front and back up (**THREE**). Different combinations stand for letters, words, or numbers.

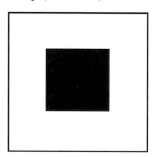 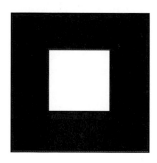 

A cipher, used for decoding messages, was made of two discs, one slightly larger than the other and pinned together in the middle so that they could be turned. One disc had letters around the edge and the other disc had numbers. By assigning each letter corresponding numbers, a signal corpsman could send a message using the flags. The code could be changed quickly by turning the discs and lining up the numbers and letters in a different way. Make your own signal flag and see if your friend can decode it.

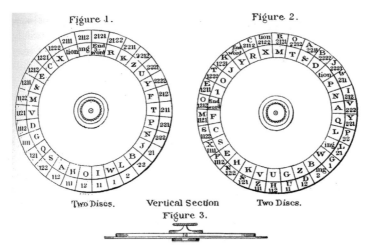

Cipher discs used by the US Signal Corps.

For the flags you will need:

- Any of the following cut into a square:
    - Paper towel
    - Piece of paper
    - Index card
- Red marker
- Straw or pencil
- Scissors

Directions:

- Draw a smaller square in the middle of your square, and color it red.
- Tape the flag to a straw or pencil.
- Use the alphabet (as shown on right) to send messages to your friends.

Wigwag Alphabet

This is the alphabet, numbers, and code signals adopted late in the war:

A = 11
B = 1221
C = 212
D = 111
E = 21
F = 1112
G = 1122
H = 211
I = 2
J = 2211
K = 1212
L = 112
M = 2112
N = 22
O = 12
P = 2121
Q = 2122
R = 122
S = 121
T = 1
U = 221
V = 2111
W = 2212
X = 1211
Y = 222
Z = 1111

1 = 12221
2 = 21112
3 = 11211
4 = 11121
5 = 11112
6 = 21111
7 = 22111
8 = 22221
9 = 22122
0 = 11111

AND = 2222
TION = 2221
ING = 1121
ED = 1222

Error = Hold flag over head and parallel to ground

Message received & cease signaling = 11, 11, 11, 3

End of word = 3
End of sentence = 33
End of message = 333

Develop Your Own Exhibit of Civil War Pictures

Description: Whether you use Flickr, PowerPoint, or a scrapbook to collect and share them, photographs can be a powerful way to tell the story of the Civil War. Historically, photography was an important development and, after Americans witnessed the carnage, it affected the way the country thought about war. Photography continues to influence, and you can create an effective visual presentation using images from Mathew Brady's art exhibit *The Dead at Antietam*, or the photographs taken by Alexander Gardner at Gettysburg. Check out the collection on the Library of Congress's website (see page 50) to get started.

Use images from the Library of Congress, a free and easy way to get great Civil War pictures.

The Gathering Storm

The Civil War may have begun in 1861, but its seeds were planted long before. From the earliest days of the United States, the North and South grew steadily apart. With a long growing season and large farms, the South focused on agriculture, growing raw materials such as cotton. Slave labor was primarily used to harvest the crops and maintain the farms or plantations.

With shorter growing seasons and a larger population, the North focused on manufacturing and producing finished products from the raw materials. Because some of the Northern states had outlawed slavery, most workers were paid.

The Union became increasingly divided between slave states and free states. Debates raged over whether new states would be free or slave and if the federal government should be the one to make this decision. For forty years, Congress made compromises on the slave status of each new state. With efforts to maintain an equal number, some new states joined the Union as free and some as slave.

Meanwhile, throughout the country people had their own opinions concerning the issue of slavery. Some identified themselves as abolitionists, or people who want to do away with slavery. One abolitionist, Harriet Beecher Stowe, wrote *Uncle Tom's Cabin*, a novel about the horrors of slavery. The novel became a best seller and raised awareness of life as a slave. However, it also created controversy; some argued that Stowe's portrayal was inaccurate.

In 1859, two years before the beginning of the war, another abolitionist, John Brown, took a more violent approach. Brown and a small group of followers raided the town of Harpers Ferry, Virginia, in hopes of capturing weapons and starting a slave rebellion. During the raid six civilians were killed and nine held hostage. A national debate ensued over Brown's actions. While most people agreed that the civilian deaths were horrible, some believed that Brown's intentions were good. Slaveholders feared slave uprisings and hated any sort of approval of Brown's mission. During his trial Brown famously stated, "I John Brown am now quite certain that the crimes of this guilty land will never be purged away; but with Blood."

Abraham Lincoln won the presidency in 1860 with a promise to halt the expansion of slavery. The South saw this as intolerable. In the winter of 1860–1861, seven slave states, beginning with South Carolina, seceded from

the Union and formed a new country, the Confederate States of America. Four
more states followed that spring.

Secede: To withdraw from something.

States and Territories of the United States of America
December 14, 1819 - March 16, 1820

Citizens pour into the streets of Savannah, Georgia.

Make Your Own Civil War Map

Description: Tens of thousands of Civil War maps have been made since the war. Some of the best can be found on the Civil War Trust website, www .civilwar.org. Creating your own will allow you to better understand the geography of the war in a personal way. Use the outline of the map below to fill in the major cities, ports, railroads, mountains, rivers, etc., all of which helped to define where and when important battles occurred. For those of you with artistic abilities, draw your own map and enjoy the process of learning!

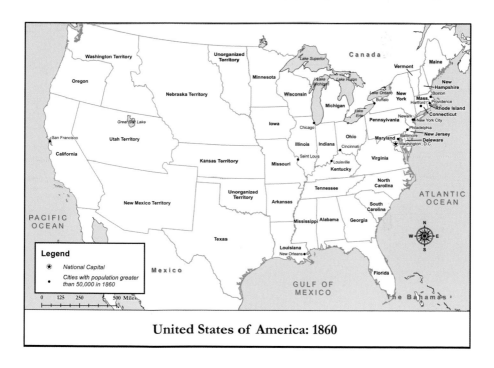

United States of America: 1860

www.civilwar.org/maps

Respond to a Letter from a Loved One

Description: If you had lived during the Civil War, it is probable that you would have sent a letter to a loved one in the field. In response, soldiers wrote as often as possible, using it as a time to reflect and connect with home.

The following letter was written to Sarah Ballou in Rhode Island from her husband, Sullivan, at Camp Clark in Washington, DC, on July 14, 1861. How would you respond if you were Sarah? If you were Sullivan's son, what would you say to him in a letter? Write a response to Sullivan either as his wife or his son.

My very dear Sarah:

The indications are very strong that we shall move in a few days—perhaps tomorrow. Lest I should not be able to write you again, I feel impelled to write lines that may fall under your eye when I shall be no more.

Our movement may be one of a few days' duration and full of pleasure—and it may be one of severe conflict and death to me. Not my will, but thine O God, be done. If it is necessary that I should

fall on the battlefield for my country, I am ready. I have no misgivings about, or lack of confidence in, the cause in which I am engaged, and my courage does not halt or falter. I know how strongly American Civilization now leans upon the triumph of the Government, and how great a debt we owe to those who went before us through the blood and suffering of the Revolution. And I am willing—perfectly willing—to lay down all my joys in this life, to help maintain this Government, and to pay that debt.

But, my dear wife, when I know that with my own joys I lay down nearly all of yours, and replace them in this life with cares and sorrows—when, after having eaten for long years the bitter fruit of orphanage myself, I must offer it as their only sustenance to my dear little children—is it weak or dishonorable, while the banner of my purpose floats calmly and proudly in the breeze, that my unbounded love for you, my darling wife and children, should struggle in fierce, though useless, contest with my love of country?

I cannot describe to you my feelings on this calm summer night, when two thousand men are sleeping around me, many of them enjoying the last, perhaps, before that of death—and I, suspicious that Death is creeping behind me with his fatal dart, am communing with God, my country, and thee . . .

But, O Sarah! If the dead can come back to this earth and flit unseen around those they loved, I shall always be near you; in the garish day and in the darkest night—amidst your happiest scenes and gloomiest hours—always, always; and if there be a soft breeze upon your cheek, it shall be my breath; or the cool air fans your throbbing temple, it shall be my spirit passing by. Sarah, do not mourn me dead; think I am gone and wait for thee, for we shall meet again.

As for my little boys, they will grow as I have done, and never know a father's love and care. Little Willie is too young to remember me long, and my blue eyed Edgar will keep my frolics with him among the dimmest memories of his childhood. Sarah, I have unlimited confidence in your maternal care and your development of their characters. Tell my two mothers his and hers I call God's blessing upon them. O Sarah, I wait for you there! Come to me, and lead thither my children.

—*Sullivan*

Soldiers of the 41st Massachusetts writing letters home.

Ballou died a week later at the First Battle of Bull Run. He was thirty-two.

Plan a Civil War Trip

Description: What is your favorite battlefield? Which battlefield would you visit if you could? Civil War battlefields can be found across the nation—from Florida to Arizona and from Minnesota to Pennsylvania. There are also many, many more Civil War sites in the form of houses, museums, cemeteries, and more. The Civil War Trust maintains an inclusive list of battlefields at www.civilwar.org/battlefields, or check out Google maps. Take the initiative, pick a battlefield, and plan out a trip. This trip can be a day trip to a local battlefield or a road trip to one farther away. Your parents will be impressed and you will be able to decide where to go and what to do.

Once you have decided where you want to go, investigate further to see what activities are offered. The National Park Service website (www.nps.gov/cwindepth) is a great place to start. Rangers usually take tours around the battlefield on a regular basis and the website often lists living history demonstrations as well. You can also check out local reenactment groups, local tourism bureaus, and the Civil War Trust's events page to help plan out your trip agenda.

Kids hiking Gettysburg National Military Park.

www.civilwar.org/battlefields

Enter the Civil War Trust
Postcard Contest

Description: How would you describe the outbreak of the Civil War and its importance today? How would you depict it in a drawing? Demonstrate your artistic and literary abilities by entering the Civil War Trust essay or postcard contests. With a different theme each year, this contest is designed to make you think about different aspects of the Civil War, such as battlefield preservation. Be creative, clear, and unique in your entry and you could win a cash prize and membership to the Civil War Trust. Winning essays are also featured in the Civil War Trust's magazine, *Hallowed Ground*. Enter to win at www.civilwar.org/contests.

Create your own postcard.

www.civilwar.org/contests

"Sew" a Housewife

Description: How many changes of clothes do you have? Most Civil War soldiers owned just one set of clothing, which was quick to wear out during long marches and bitter fighting. As you can imagine, mending clothes was a must for soldiers. Therefore, most Civil War soldiers carried a "housewife," or sewing kit. This aptly named sewing kit contained the items necessary to darn socks, replace buttons, or fix a hole in a jacket. Made for soldiers by wives, mothers, daughters, and friends, housewives were crafted from scraps of leftover fabric and typically included buttons, needles, thread, and extra fabric. When it was time to replace a button or stitch a tear, a soldier could quickly pull out his housewife, and all the necessary supplies would be there.

Directions:

1. Cut a piece of paper into a rectangle using the measurements given below.

2. Fold your rectangle into thirds as the pattern below shows.

3. In the boxes labeled pocket, draw in items that would commonly be found in a housewife. See the photo below for one housewife example.

4. On the other side of the paper, draw and color in a pattern that would typically be found on a piece of scrap fabric. Examples include plaid, floral, or stripes.

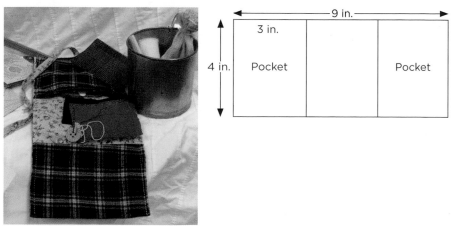

Contents of a housewife commonly included needle, thread, pieces of fabric, and buttons.

Quiz Your Friends on the Civil War

Description: How many soldiers fought in the Civil War? What were the bloodiest battles? How much were soldiers paid? Do you know the answers to these questions? Stump your friends and family members by creating your own questions and quizzing them on your favorite facts about the Civil War. If you need a little help with questions try the Civil War Trust's education page, where you can find a list of the Civil War's most frequently asked questions, as well as Name That Battlefield quizzes.

Use your Civil War knowledge to stump your friends.

www.civilwar.org/namethatbattlefield

Write Emancipation Proclamation Poetry

Description: On September 22, 1862, Abraham Lincoln issued the Preliminary Emancipation Proclamation, granting freedom to the slaves in areas rebelling against the Union. The proclamation took effect on January 1, 1863. On May 22, 1863, the War Department issued General Order 143, creating the United States Colored Troops (USCT), allowing African-Americans the opportunity to fight for their own freedom, which they did in great numbers. In honor of these monumental acts, write an acrostic poem using EMANCIPATE. We've started the first two lines for you below.

Enslaved
My Freedom
A
N
C
I
P
A
T
E

Lady Liberty, a symbol of liberty, holds the Emancipation Proclamation.

Emancipation

In September 1862, following one of the deadliest battles in American history, the Battle of Antietam, President Abraham Lincoln issued the Preliminary Emancipation Proclamation.

The Emancipation Proclamation, while believed by many to have freed the slaves, actually only granted freedom to the slaves in some of the Confederate States. Lincoln stated, "... I do order and declare that all persons held as slaves within said designated States, and parts of States, are, and henceforward shall be free ..."

Following the proclamation, many slaves left their owners and went north or followed Union soldiers as they moved through the South. Because slaves were considered property by their owners, the Union deemed the slaves contraband, property that could be taken during a time of war. Once north or with the Union Army, they were no longer enslaved and were considered free by the Union.

Refugees coming into Union lines at New Bern, North Carolina.

Life was incredibly difficult for former slaves. Many did not have a place to live, a way to make money to support their families, or the ability to read or write. Traveling north or with the Union army was dangerous; there was always a risk of being captured, injured, or getting sick.

In addition to freeing the slaves, the Emancipation Proclamation stated that ". . . persons of suitable condition, will be received into the armed service of the United States." African Americans could now serve in the Union Army. Two months after the Proclamation, the War Department sanctioned the creation of the United States Colored Troops (USCT), and colored units began to be integrated into the army.

By the end of the war, more than 200,000, African-American men, many former slaves, volunteered. Nearly 40,000 gave their lives for the cause.

Emancipation: The act of setting someone free.
Proclamation: A public announcement.

USCT in South Carolina.

Draw a Civil War Monument

Description: Monuments provide a place for the living to pay their respects and remember the sacrifices made by others. Meant to last a long time, they often include the names of those involved, a symbol of the group being honored, a date or other information about the event, and are typically made out of a stone or metal. From the end of the war to today people and organizations have memorialized the fallen by constructing thousands of monuments across the country.

You can honor those sacrifices as well by sketching your own rendering of an existing monument or by creating your own design. Research the Civil War history of your hometown or state and draw a monument that inspires reflection and honors the sacrifices of the soldiers.

Monument to the volunteer firefighters of New York City at Gettysburg.

Compose a "Then and Now" Photo

Description: Photography was a relatively new technology at the beginning of the Civil War. It was used to document the war, and pictures of Civil War battlefields could be seen by the public for the first time. During the war some of the era's most famous photographers made their names taking pictures of generals, soldiers, and battlefields.

Create your own "Then and Now" photograph. Choose a picture from the Civil War, stage your own version that imitates it, then snap a photo. You don't have to be in the exact same spot as the original picture. Just gather some friends and set it up to look the same. Or find a location that looks similar. Remember, the process you follow is a lot simpler than that of the Civil War soldiers and photographers. If you are feeling ambitious, research the photographic process of the time to find out just how difficult it was.

Then and now: The Ray Family Farm at Wilson's Creek Battlefield, Missouri.

Construct a Pup Tent

Description: Creating a tent in your bedroom or living room is always fun. But if you consider that a Civil War soldier's pup tent was often all he had keeping him from the rain, cold, snow, and sun it might not sound like so much fun anymore. Each Union soldier was issued half of a tent. This rectangular piece of canvas was then hooked to another soldier's half to create an A-frame pup tent meant to sleep two. Soldiers often referred to them as "dog tents" because they were better suited for a dog and were not very effective at keeping out the weather. However, the tents could be set up anywhere by using a rifle with a bayonet as a pole and they were much better than nothing, which is what most Confederate soldiers had.

Using a few sheets or blankets as well as some chairs, drape the fabric so that it resembles a tent like the ones below. Hint: Use clothespins to help secure the fabric.

Pup tents pitched during a reenactment.

Assemble Lincoln's Stovepipe Hat

Description: The life and legacy of Abraham Lincoln is well known to most Americans. The fortitude with which Lincoln fought the Civil War, the significance of the Emancipation Proclamation, and the gentleness of his ideas of reunification place him alongside our greatest presidents. Possibly the best-known aspect of Abraham Lincoln's image is that of his top hat, in which it is said he often carried legal papers and letters. Assembling a stovepipe hat in honor of our sixteenth president is an easy task and one that you can share with your friends and siblings. Just follow the instructions below.

Materials:
- 7-inch paper plate
- black paint or marker
- 2 sheets of black, 9 x 12-inch construction paper
- paintbrush (optional)
- glue
- tape
- scissors

Allan Pinkerton, Abraham Lincoln, and Gen. McClernand.

Directions:

1. Paint or color the paper plate black. Allow to dry.

2. Cut out the center of the plate, leaving an outside rim about two inches thick for the brim of the hat.

3. Place the two sheets of construction paper side-by-side vertically so that the longest sides of the paper are touching and tape or glue together.

4. Cut ½-inch slits along the bottom of the construction paper, about one inch apart.

5. Roll up the construction paper so that the two remaining sides touch, and glue or tape together so that you have a long cylindrical tube.

6. Fold the slits out at a 90-degree angle.

7. Place the tube, slit side down, on top of the plate and glue down. You may find it helpful to weigh the tube down with several sheets of paper in order to allow the glue enough time to dry.

Perform

Sometimes the best way to learn about the past is to actually experience what life would have been like at that time. In this section you will participate in activities that get you involved with life during the Civil War. Try on Civil War–style clothing, play a fife or drum, do the rebel yell, and reenact part of a battle.

There are people known as reenactors or living historians who teach others about the past by reenacting a historic event or pretending as though they are living at a certain time in history. Rather than just reading about the life of a soldier during the Civil War they will actually put on Civil War–era clothing and participate in activities such as sleeping in a tent or fighting in a make-believe battle.

There is a great deal to be learned by walking in someone else's shoes. Use your imagination to go back in time and have fun.

Model a Uniform or Period Dress

Description: How did Civil War soldiers stay cool on hot summer days in those uniforms made of wool? How did nineteenth-century women maneuver in those big hoop dresses? Find out for yourself by dressing like a Civil War soldier or civilian. Contact a reenactment/historical unit in your area for help—you'll feel closer to and get a better understanding of the Civil War period by dressing as they did back then.

Visit a Local Civil War Monument

Description: By visiting a monument, you will not only honor the memory of the soldiers and sailors who served in the Civil War, you will also learn something new. Many cities and towns, especially those east of the Mississippi River, erected monuments to honor those who contributed to the war effort. The number and distribution of these monuments is in itself a testament to the commitment that was made by nearly every community over the course of the conflict. Visiting your local monument can be your way of paying homage to the people who sacrificed so much to take part in America's defining struggle. Reading the many names inscribed in stone can be a powerful experience. Go see the names written there (you may even recognize some of them) and remember the deeds they performed so long ago. That's why the monuments were built.

One of the many monuments at the Vicksburg National Military Park.

Play a Drum, Bugle, or Fife

Description: Musicians were an important part of Civil War life. They served as a means of communication in camp and on the battlefield. Drummers, buglers, and occasionally fifers called men to meals, to battle, set a rhythm for marching, and provided comfort through some of the hardest times. Buglers had to memorize forty-nine separate calls and drummers thirty-nine different beats. Give it a shot and see if you would have made a good Civil War musician.

Members of the 93rd New York Infantry Drum Corps, photographed at Bealton, Virginia, August 1863.

Life at War

Inspired to fight by a sense of patriotism, the chance for adventure, and steady pay, the average Yankee or Rebel tended to be white, born in the United States, a farmer, unmarried, and between the ages of eighteen and twenty-nine. He stood about 5 feet 8 inches tall and weighed about 143 pounds.

When young men joined the army they were assigned to a regiment with other men from around their hometown. The men were issued their equipment, which commonly included their uniform, a hat, a bag called a haversack, their musket, ammunition, a blanket, and food. Soldiers would add personal items such as pictures, cards, a toothbrush, razor, and soap. All of the equipment could weigh close to fifty pounds.

Once organized and prepared with their gear, the regiments were then given their assignments. Soldiers on both sides spent the majority of their time marching and drilling. Battles were not a common occurrence;

A group of Union soldiers prepare a meal in camp.

Men recover at a hospital near Fredericksburg, Virginia, after the Battle of the Wilderness.

some soldiers even hoped for a battle in order to relieve the boredom of life in the army. Private Oliver Willcox Norton of the 83rd Pennsylvania Infantry once said, "First thing in the morning is drill, then drill, then drill again. Then drill, drill, a little more drill. Then drill and lastly drill. Between drills, we drill. . . ."

When they were not drilling, soldiers passed the time writing letters; playing games like checkers, dominoes, and poker; whittling; making music; and praying. One soldier summed it up when he wrote to his wife, "Soldiering is 99 percent boredom and 1 percent sheer terror."

When battles finally took place they were indescribably horrifying. With the new weaponry, such as rifled muskets that could propel a bullet farther and more accurately, combined with tactics such as marching in a long line toward the enemy, death was common and gruesome. Wounds from battle were often untreatable, causing slow and painful deaths. Those who survived were left to bury the bodies.

Yankee: Union soldier.
Rebel: Confederate soldier.

Do the Rebel Yell

Description: High pitch, low pitch, whoop, yip, yell, and scream! Do it! Just let it go. The Confederate soldiers did and succeeded in boosting their own morale. Most importantly they put the fear of battle in the Union soldiers before it even started. Nobody really knows where it started and there are as many calls or styles as there were soldiers. Have fun with your yell and imagine how scary it would be to hear it coming from thousands of men on the other side of the battlefield!

Hear an Example:
There are several videos on YouTube that demonstrate the rebel yell. One in particular, titled "Rare Footage of Civil War Veterans Doing the Rebel Yell," is a 1930 recording of Confederate veterans.

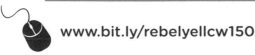 **www.bit.ly/rebelyellcw150**

Hike a Civil War Battlefield

Description: Walk to the left flank of the 20th Maine at Gettysburg or take a stroll through the Hornets' Nest at Shiloh. Hiking a battlefield can give you a true sense of the factors that influenced the outcome of a battle. Getting a feel for the scale and terrain of a battlefield is a great way to gain a deeper understanding of the events that occurred there.

A peaceful footpath on the Shiloh Battlefield, where many soldiers "saw the elephant" for the first time.

Send a Letter to a Soldier

Description: Communication in the twenty-first century is instantaneous and often visual. E-mail, video conferencing, and text messages make it remarkably easy to stay in touch with friends and loved ones. During the war, letter writing was the easiest and most common form of communication. Civil War soldiers often passed the time writing letters and were overjoyed to receive letters from home. While communication was not as fast as it is today, letters were the one connection for soldiers and their families during those four long years.

Imagine you can communicate with a Civil War soldier. Choose a soldier and write him a letter. Be sincere. Ask him what it was like. Tell him how much you appreciate his sacrifice and the things you like best about studying the war. You may want to take it a step further and choose a soldier from your hometown or state.

There are several things you can do with the letter once you have it written. With the many activities set to commemorate the 150th anniversary of the Civil War, your local newspaper may be interested in printing your letter as part of an article on the commemoration or even as a letter to the editor. You can also send the letter to the Civil War Trust. Since Civil War soldiers were often very young, you might also consider putting the letter away until you reach the age of the soldier you have chosen to write to—it won't be very long. Whatever you choose to do, try to imagine how your soldier might have felt upon receiving this letter.

Sing "John Brown's Body"

Description: On the morning of October 17, 1859, John Brown, a staunch abolitionist, and a group of his supporters seized the federal armory and arsenal in Harper's Ferry, Virginia, hoping that the local slave population would rise up and revolt. This was not to be. The standoff ended with the death of several local residents, as well as some of Brown's own followers.

The nation was divided over his actions. Many abolitionists called him a hero, while slaveholders called him a villain. Found guilty of treason, murder, and conspiring with slaves to rebel, John Brown was sentenced to death and hanged on December 2, 1859. Before he died, Brown issued these final, seemingly prophetic, words in a note he handed to his jailer:

Charlestown, VA, 2ⁿᵈ, December, 1859

I John Brown am now quite certain that the crimes of this guilty, land will never be purged away; but with Blood.

A year later, the first Southern state seceded from the Union and John Brown's actions were immortalized in a song popular among Union troops during the Civil War—"John Brown's Body," sung to the tune of the soon-to-be-written "Battle Hymn of the Republic." We've included the lyrics on the next page. Sing along!

John Brown: "The meteor of the war."

John Brown's Body
Library of Congress

John Brown's body lies a-mouldering in the grave;
John Brown's body lies a-mouldering in the grave;
John Brown's body lies a-mouldering in the grave;
His soul's marching on!

(Chorus)
Glory, glory, hallelujah! Glory, glory, hallelujah!
Glory, glory, hallelujah! His soul's marching on!

He's gone to be a soldier in the army of the Lord!
He's gone to be a soldier in the army of the Lord!
He's gone to be a soldier in the army of the Lord!
His soul's marching on!

(Chorus)

John Brown's knapsack is strapped upon his back!
John Brown's knapsack is strapped upon his back!
John Brown's knapsack is strapped upon his back!
His soul's marching on!

(Chorus)

His pet lambs will meet him on the way;
His pet lambs will meet him on the way;
His pet lambs will meet him on the way;
They go marching on!

(Chorus)

They will hang Jeff Davis to a sour apple tree!
They will hang Jeff Davis to a sour apple tree!
They will hang Jeff Davis to a sour apple tree!
As they march along!

(Chorus)

Now, three rousing cheers for the Union;
Now, three rousing cheers for the Union;
Now, three rousing cheers for the Union;
As we are marching on!

Preserve a Battlefield

Description: Battlefields are part of our national heritage, scenes of struggle and sacrifice where American soldiers lost their lives. Battlefields allow us to learn the history of war by going to the place where it actually happened. They are places where everyone is welcome to go to reflect in his or her own way. Numerous organizations, including the Civil War Trust, save and protect battlefields. You can get involved too. You can help by writing letters to elected officials, lending your voice at meetings, making calls, raising money, or cleaning up a park. Visit the Trust's website at www.civilwar.org to find out more.

Park Day Volunteers on the Lick Run Battlefield.

 **www.civilwar.org**

Pick Your Favorite General

Description: The following generals (and admiral) are just a few of those who experienced both great success and tremendous defeat during America's most devastating war. Match the biographies to the general in the chart below and decide which is your favorite. Then, look up your favorite and find a famous quote. Perform the quote the way you think your general would have. Feel free to choose someone who is not on the list below. If you want to see more commanders, the Civil War Trust's biographies page (www.civilwar.org/biographies) includes more than 130 officer bios; check it out and decide which officer interests you the most.

1. Thomas "Stonewall" Jackson _____	**A.** This general was known as Sam and served as captain during the Mexican War, winning citations for gallantry and bravery. During the Civil War he experienced triumphs at Forts Henry and Donelson, earning himself national notoriety and the attention of President Lincoln, who later named him general-in-chief of the Armies of the United States. He aggressively attacked at the Wilderness, Spotsylvania, Cold Harbor, and Petersburg battlefields, and he accepted the surrender of Robert E. Lee at Appomattox Court House.
2. Joseph Johnston _____	**B.** This general was a descendant of a Revolutionary War hero and distinguished himself both at the United States Military Academy (West Point) and in the Army Corps of Engineers. At the beginning of the Civil War his reputation earned him an offer from Abraham Lincoln to command the Federal forces. After declining this offer, he went on to command Confederate forces with great success and distinction. However, after a relentless and bloody campaign, the well-supplied Federals forced the surrender of his army on April 9, 1865.
3. David Farragut _____	**C.** This general was sixth in his class at West Point and went on to serve in Florida during the Second Seminole War. The years before the Civil War found him working in a variety of positions including superintendent of the Louisiana Military Academy. Despite his love for the South, he joined the ranks of the Union army because of his hatred of secession. Although he experienced many of the battles of the war, he is best known for his famous march. He received the surrender of Joseph E. Johnston in February 1865.

www.civilwar.org/biographies

4. Ulysses S. Grant	**D.** This general graduated from West Point and before the war taught at Virginia Military Institute. In the first years of the Civil War, this general was extremely successful because of his high expectations for his troops and his leadership style. He earned his well-known nickname at the First Battle of Manassas and went on to successes in the Shenandoah Valley, Second Manassas, and Fredericksburg among others. After his victory at Chancellorsville, he was wounded by friendly fire and died eight days later from pneumonia. To this day he is remembered as a great military hero and continues to maintain celebrity status.
5. Robert E. Lee	**E.** This vice admiral in the Federal Navy was born and raised in the South, but was to become one of the most successful Union Naval officers of the Civil War. Although only twelve years old, he took part in the War of 1812 and proved his abilities as a sailor. Early in the Civil War, he took control of the city and port of New Orleans and went on to win the Battle of Mobile Bay where he made his famous statement, "Damn the torpedoes! Full speed ahead!" He defeated the Confederates and took control of the last open seaport on the Gulf of Mexico.
6. William Tecumseh Sherman	**F.** This general attended West Point and served with honors in the Mexican War, the Seminole Wars, and as quartermaster general in California. Upon his resignation from the US Army at the beginning of the Civil War, he was appointed brigadier general in the Confederacy. He defended Richmond during McClellan's Peninsula Campaign but was wounded in the Battle of Seven Pines. Robert E. Lee succeeded him. After recovery, he commanded forces in the Western Theater and would eventually withdraw from Sherman as he made his "March to the Sea." He was forced to surrender the Army of Tennessee to Sherman in April of 1865 and went on to serve as a US Congressman.

Answers: 1:D, 2:F, 3:E, 4:A, 5:B, 6:C

My favorite general or admiral is _____

because _____

_____

Hold a Piece of History

Description: Holding something that was held 150 years ago can connect you with the past and act as a sort of time machine. More than 620,000 lives were lost in the Civil War and holding a bullet found on a battlefield or a rifle used by one of its brave soldiers can allow you to understand the reality of the past in a way that very few other things can. You will not be able to hold all historical items. Time has eaten away at some of the more fragile items, and oils from your skin can further damage items like paper. However, there are plenty of artifacts from this time period that you can wrap your fingers around, such as bullets, belt buckles, and cannonballs. Visit your local museum or historical sites where they often have items set aside for just such purposes.

Boy holding Union and Confederate bullets found on the Perryville Battlefield, c. 1927.

The Home Front

Almost every family had a son, husband, brother, or father away at war. For those who remained at home, the Civil War changed their lives forever.

With so many men at war, women had to take on more responsibility at home, doing work that their husbands and sons would normally have done. In the South, women on plantations took charge, serving as plantation mistresses and managing slaves. In the North, women took positions in factories at manufacturing jobs. Women on both sides also took on back-breaking household chores while making clothing and supplies for their loved ones at war.

Women were not the only ones to take over the work. Children also became more involved with tasks that were once the responsibility of their older siblings or fathers. Some children even traveled with the army as drummer boys.

A reenactor recreates a common scene on the home front.

The war was most difficult for those in the South, where most battles were fought. Women and children could be caught in a battle taking place near their homes; in some cases bullets came through windows or hit walls. Often the armies would take over civilians' homes to use as hospitals, forcing the family to move out or live in the basement. Following a battle, cleanup would become the responsibility of the civilians; this included burying the dead.

Part of the Union's strategy for winning the war was to block incoming shipments of supplies and to destroy factories that supported the Confederate war effort. Union and Confederate soldiers would take food and livestock from civilians as they moved through the South. As the war progressed, food, jobs, and money began to diminish and the people at home suffered. At one point, Southern women rioted in the Confederate capital, demanding food for their families in what came to be known as the "bread riots."

Unionist southern refugees leaving the old homestead.

Reenact with Your Friends

Description: Reenacting is the practice of dressing in historically correct clothing and re-creating a battle or other scene from history. Some reenactors will even eat historically correct food and speak as if they were living in the past.

Attending a real reenactment can be fun, but donning a Civil War uniform and staging your own reenactment can be even more so. Pick a battle and research the strategies used by its generals to stage your own battle, complete with flank marches, rebel yells, and reconnaissance. Then decide who will portray the Confederates and who will portray the Yankees, as well as who will "command" each side.

The average Civil War soldier was a private whose main job was to do what he was ordered to do. Those in command should be able to direct the soldiers to their proper locations on the battlefield and tell them when and where to advance. You might want to decide ahead of your "battle" who will pretend to "die" or be "wounded." Sometimes reenactors will draw lots to figure this out before they begin. If you can find some clothing that looks like a Civil War uniform, or perhaps a hat, be sure to wear it. It will help to make your experience more realistic.

As you take the field and prepare to go into battle, try to imagine what it was like for the real soldiers—what were they seeing, hearing, feeling? What would it be like if you had real bullets coming at you? If you are designated to be "wounded," think about what was going through a soldier's mind as he lay there on the field. Hopefully your experience will bring you closer to the real soldiers' experience during the war.

Young reenactors prepare to drum their comrades into battle at Spotsylvania.

Whistle "Dixie" or "Yankee Doodle"

Description: Music played an important role in the movement and entertainment of Civil War troops. Instruments and bands of all types were used to help keep the pace and to keep spirits lifted on long marches. Uneventful days and nights between battles and marches were spent singing and listening to bands. Two of the most popular songs were "Dixie" and "Yankee Doodle." "Dixie" found great popularity in 1859 when it became part of the traveling blackface minstrel shows. The origins of "Yankee Doodle" date back to the French and Indian War, when British soldiers sang it to mock their unsophisticated American counterparts. You can demonstrate your own musical ability by whistling one, or both, of the songs. See if you can sing them as well. The words are on the following page.

To find samples of the music on Wikipedia, simply search: "Dixie, the Song" for Dixie and "Yankee Doodle Song" for Yankee Doodle.

"Dixie," written by a northerner, became the anthem of the Southern Confederacy.

www.wikipedia.com

Dixie

I wish I was in the land of cotton,
Old times they are not forgotten;
Look away! Look away! Look away! Dixie Land.
In Dixie Land where I was born,
Early on one frosty mornin',
Look away! Look away! Look away! Dixie Land.

Yankee Doodle

(Chorus)
Yankee Doodle went to town
A-riding on a pony.
He stuck a feather in his hat
And called it macaroni.
Yankee Doodle, keep it up,
Yankee Doodle dandy,
Mind the music and the step,
and with the girls be handy!

Father and I went down to camp,
Along with Captain Gooding,
And there we saw the men and boys,
As thick as hasty pudding.

(Chorus)

And there was Captain Washington,
And gentle folks about him.
They say he's grown so tarnal proud,
He will not ride without them.

(Chorus)

Play Capture the Flag

Description: The regimental flag or "colors" played an enormously important role on the battlefield. Held by soldiers who were called color bearers, regimental flags were positioned at the center of a regiment for all to see. While in the midst of a terrifying and confusing battle, soldiers used the flag to maintain position and formation. Seeing their colors waving above the insanity of battle, soldiers gained a sense of their whereabouts and renewed their spirits.

Because of the flag's significance, losing the regimental flag in battle was one of the worst things that could happen; however, capturing the enemy's flag in battle was one of the best things that could happen.

A friendly game of Capture the Flag with your friends can help you understand the significance of the flag. In your game, obtaining and protecting the "flag" is the objective and symbolically represents the importance of the flag to the Civil War soldier on the battlefield. The rules of Capture the Flag differ from location to location, but the objective is always the same—capture the other team's flag.

Rules:
1. Find an appropriate location. This is usually a field of some sort, but can be either indoor or outdoor.

2. Divide the field into two distinct "territories."

3. Divide into two groups with each taking possession of one territory.

4. Each side needs a flag, which is most often a piece of fabric, but can be any object small enough to be carried. Glow sticks are fun to use at night.

5. Each team should hide its flag according to established rules of visibility. Example: The flag needs to be in something green or under a large rock.

6. The object of the game is for each team to make its way into the opposing team's territory, grab the flag, and return to its own territory without being tagged, or touched by an opposing player.

7. Players are safe within their own territory.

8. The flag may be defended by tagging opposing players who attempt to take it.

As a group, you will need to decide which set of rules you will follow once a person has been captured or "tagged." Perhaps you could research the prisoner exchange system used during the Civil War and create your own rules accordingly.

The Assault on Fort Sanders (Kurz & Allison).

Find

As time goes by, things get lost, put away in out-of-reach places, or forgotten. Think about a toy or stuffed animal you had as a little kid that you have since put away. This is part of your history and it still exists, but it has been moved and is no longer part of your daily thoughts. Maybe someday you will find that toy and it will bring back memories of your past.

Historians work to piece together the past and often this means finding objects, papers, or memories. These items or memories are not gone, they just need to be found and put together in the correct order.

In this section you will need to be a history detective. You must find the locations of sunken ships, break secret codes, and uncover the mystery of an unknown soldier.

As you embark upon this journey, you'll learn some of the most important lessons of the Civil War.

Browse Civil War Images at the Library of Congress

Description: Go to the Library of Congress website at www.loc.gov, click "Library Catalogs," click "Prints and Photographs," click "Civil War," and have at it. Photography was relatively new at the time of the Civil War, making it the first war to be widely photographed. The Library of Congress is home to more than 9,000 Civil War images created throughout, and shortly after, the Civil War. You can either browse or search the photographs within each collection. Look at battlefields, soldiers, the living and the dead, scarred landscapes, cities burned and ravaged, and every other subject Civil War imagery has to offer.

The Library of Congress is free to use and has thousands of pictures.

www.loc.gov

Complete the Weapons Exhibit

Description: The Civil War is often referred to as the first modern war because it included the most advanced technology and innovations for warfare at the time. Mass production of war materials, rifling of gun barrels, and the use of the minié ball are just a few of the technological advancements that made this the deadliest war in American history. The Union army issued approximately four million weapons during the Civil War, which does not even count the almost 8,000 pieces of artillery. Some of the most widely used weapons of the war are below.

One of the jobs of historians is to put together or curate exhibits. This means finding objects and writing descriptions to help people learn about a certain topic. In this case, the descriptions are provided; your job is to find the objects. Using the information provided, find images of the weapons and ammunition. Cut and paste the images into the correct descriptions on a grid like the one below.

1853 Enfield Rifle	.577 caliber	Second most widely used infantry weapon next to the Springfield.
1861 Springfield Rifle	.58 caliber	Most widely used shoulder arm in both armies. Favored for its accuracy, range, and reliability.
1860 Colt Army Revolver	.44 caliber	Most popular handgun in Union Army.
Colt 1851 Navy Revolver	.36 caliber	Preferred handgun in Confederate Army.
Sharps Rifle	.52 caliber	Popular for long range and high accuracy.
Parrott Rifled Cannon	2.9- and 3.0-inch artillery shell	Came in different sizes, but the 10-20 pounders were the most prevalent.

New Technology

From weaponry to transportation, communications to medicine, the Civil War brought a surge of new ideas that changed warfare and life from that point forward.

Weaponry

Before the Civil War, soldiers carried smoothbore muskets, which rarely hit what they were supposed to hit and only at short range. Therefore, armies commonly fought in straight lines at short distances from one another. During the Civil War, the newly invented rifled musket had longer range and better accuracy. This ultimately brought on a new style of combat that included the use of trenches.

Balloons, ironclad ships, and submarines were first used in combat during the Civil War. Balloons, which looked like today's hot air balloons, were used by the Union army for watching Confederate movements at long distances. Ironclads were ships encased in iron. The Union and Confederate navies used these iron-clad warships and it changed naval warfare forever. The Confederacy also built a submarine, the first of its kind to successfully torpedo and sink an enemy ship.

Transportation

The Civil War became the first war in which railroads played a critical and decisive role. Both armies used railroads to move troops and supplies to and from the front. Having available rail lines during a battle or siege offered a huge advantage. After the war many veterans worked on building the rail line for the

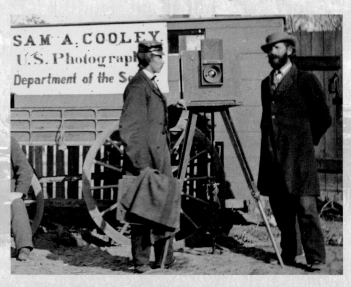

Two photographers pose with their instrument.

First Transcontinental Railroad, which connected railways from one end of the country to the other.

Communication

The electric telegraph, which sent messages in Morse code (see illustration) through wires, had been invented as a means of long-distance communication a few years prior to the war. During the war, the telegraph provided instantaneous communication between the armies and their capitals and with other friendly forces, allowing for information on supplies, enemy positions, and the issuing of orders. The telegraph also allowed for news of the war to quickly reach citizens at home. By the end of the war the armies had installed more than 15,000 miles of telegraph wire.

A man operates a telegraph machine in this *Harpers Weekly* illustration.

Photography

The invention of the wet-plate process, which, unlike older photograph-developing processes, produced a glass negative that allowed for images to be easily and inexpensively reproduced on light-sensitive paper. Photographers traveled with the armies, capturing images of war and its consequences. Their photos serve as a record of the war.

Medicine

Before the Civil War, medicine in the United States was amateur at best. There was limited understanding of germs and infection, and a lack of resources for effective treatment. During the war, men who served as doctors in the army received "on the job" training. Over the course of the war, developments in record-keeping, triage, cleanliness, nursing, and medical training shaped medicine into what we know today.

Range: The farthest distance from which a gun can shoot a bullet.
Triage: The process of deciding the level of treatment for sick or injured people.

Look Up "Sherman's Neckties"

Description: William T. Sherman's March to the Sea is often considered to be among the first examples of "total war." Making his way through Georgia and later through South Carolina and North Carolina, Sherman and his men wreaked havoc on the people of the South, hoping to destroy their will as well as their ability to fight. In their wake, Union troops left heaps of what came to be known as "Sherman's Neckties." Search this phrase on the Internet and find out what they were.

Union General William T. Sherman.

Research Soldiers' Causes of Death

Description: Life was dangerous for Civil War soldiers. Surgeons did the best they could in the field hospitals, but they did not know about tiny germs they could not see and they didn't have the resources for cleanliness on the battlefield. Most wounds suffered by Civil War soldiers were to the arms and legs and amputation was the wounded soldier's best chance of survival. In fact, three-fourths of a surgeon's time was spent amputating limbs. The closer to the torso a wound was, the higher the death rate. Therefore, wounds to the stomach led to almost certain death, while wounds on the appendages could be treated with amputation. The sooner the amputation was performed, the better the chance of survival. If amputation was delayed more than forty-eight hours, blood poisoning, bone infection, or gangrene would set in, and the death rate doubled. Doctors used chloroform and ether for anesthesia.

Danger was not only found on the battlefield. Close quarters and unsanitary conditions, including contaminations from dead bodies and human waste, led to an assortment of diseases and death. Unfortunately, treatment options were often as dangerous as the diseases themselves and death from sickness was prevalent. Read about the illnesses and then do your own triage on the soldiers listed on the following page.

Soldier's cemetery in Alexandria, Virginia.

Here are some common Civil War diseases:

Dysentery	Number one killer during the Civil War. Victims get severe diarrhea with passage of mucous and blood.
Typhoid Fever	"Camp Fever" was the number two killer and was transmitted by body lice. This disease causes a high fever, intense headache, intense rash, and delirium.
Ague	Pronounced "AY-gyu." A high fever with a cycle of chills and sweating. Also known as, "swamp fever."
Yellow Fever	Caused by a virus, this disease is carried by a specific mosquito and can be fatal.
Malaria	Spread by mosquitoes. Symptoms include shaking, high fever, chills, and other flu-like symptoms.
Scurvy	Disease caused by a lack of vitamin C. The gums get spongy and bleed; teeth become loose.
Pneumonia	Disease causing inflammation of the lungs.
Tuberculosis	A very contagious disease that is caused by bacteria. It mainly affects the lungs.
Smallpox	An extremely dangerous, contagious disease that causes fever and "bumps" similar to chickenpox.
Other	chicken pox, scarlet fever, measles, mumps, and whooping cough

The following soldiers are sick. Read their symptoms and use the chart above to determine a diagnosis.

Name	Symptoms	What Is the Disease?
Preston Soule	Mr. Soule presents with a very high fever and a severe rash. He is delirious and rambles.	
Albert Eddy	Albert Eddy has been stationed in the low-land swamps of South Carolina. He shakes violently and burns with fever.	
George Gammons	George Gammons came to the infirmary with alternating chills and fever.	
Daniel Handy	Mr. Handy is dehydrated because of his diarrhea, which is often bloody.	
Noah Davis	Noah Davis's gums are bleeding profusely and his teeth are starting to fall out.	

Discover the Civil War in Your Hometown

Description: Have you ever wondered what it would be like to pick up a book that your great-great-great grandfather read, or to hold the comb of one of your ancestors? Or even the journal of one of the founders of the town you live in? Many communities have a wealth of historic documents and artifacts in local libraries and museums.

Check out the special collections sections of your local library. Look for rare books, military collections, oral histories, genealogies, and family histories. Talk to the experts; historians, librarians, and volunteers may have some secret info. Find out how your hometown was involved in the Civil War. Don't be surprised if it played an important role.

Letters, photos, and equipment can be found in your town.

Match the Equipment

Description: Although supply shortages plagued both sides throughout the war, soldiers were issued certain equipment upon their enlistment. These items were often supplemented by personal items that lessened the hardships of soldiering. Common soldiers had to carry whatever they wanted to take along with them, so these items had to be small, lightweight, and personally significant enough to be worth carrying hundreds of miles and into battle.

Test your knowledge and see if you can match the items with the description of their use.

1. Canteen

2. Silverware

3. Razor

4. Playing cards

5. Photographs

6. Bible

7. Haversack

8. Rations

9. Musket or rifle

A. All soldiers were issued this item, similar to a backpack, but with one shoulder strap. It was used to carry rations and personal items. _____

B. Although these items differed between the Union and Confederacy, salted meat, hardtack, dried corn and beans, and coffee were common items. _____

C. Many soldiers carried these items in their haversacks to help them remember loved ones they had left at home. _____

D. All soldiers were issued this item, although there were many varieties. Some of the most common were the 1861 Springfield and the 1853 Enfield. _____

E. Civil War soldiers had a lot of time of their hands. While drilling and fighting were their primary objectives, during downtime, some played a variety of games using these. _____

F. Some soldiers carried this type of personal item to help keep well groomed while at war. _____

G. These items were sometimes issued to soldiers to assist them in the preparation and consumption of their meals. _____

H. This item was typically carried over the shoulder. It was sometimes insulated with cloth to keep the contents cool and the metal from being punctured. It was used to carry water. _____

I. For spiritual enhancement, many soldiers read this. _____

Answers: 1:H, 2:G, 3:F, 4:E, 5:C, 6:I, 7:A, 8:B, 9:D

Uncover Franklin Thompson's Real Name

Description: Franklin Thompson was not like other Civil War soldiers. On May 25, 1861, at the age of twenty, Franklin was mustered into the 2nd Michigan Infantry. After working as a nurse during several of the first battles of the war, it is rumored that Mr. Thompson spent some time as a spy for the Union army. Although this was never confirmed, Franklin's memoirs detail several exploits from behind enemy lines throughout the war. But Franklin had another secret. Research Franklin Thompson to discover the secret.

Who was Franklin Thompson?

Locate Someone Connected to the Civil War

Description: The Civil War touched the lives of every American at the time and for a long time thereafter. Because of the magnitude of the Civil War and the impact it had on individual lives, historians have conducted a great deal of research on it. If you look, you are likely to find some personal connection. You may find a great-great-great grandfather who fought at Gettysburg or Shiloh; or you may find your neighbor's grandfather arrived in America during Reconstruction, a very difficult time as communities attempted to rebuild and redefine themselves. Whatever the case, a visit to your local library or historical society can begin a journey that will take you places you never expected.

"Telling the story of Gettysburg," c. 1892.

In the News

During the war there was no television, Internet, or phone service. News traveled mainly through newspapers and letters and was much slower than it is today.

Printed daily or weekly, newspapers served as the main source of information. Soldiers and civilians alike kept up on what was happening through the newspaper. Reports from journalists on the front provided firsthand accounts of battles while editorials provided opinions on the course of the war.

As with most conflicts, people had differing opinions; some people wanted the Union and Confederacy to compromise while some wanted the war to end only when the country was reunited. The way information was presented in the newspapers, either in support of the war or against it, would affect public opinion. President Lincoln, other politicians, and a few generals used this fact and the press to help promote their goals.

Newspapers at the time consisted mainly of text; however, there were some images including illustrations and engravings that were made from photographs. Actual photographs could not be used in newspapers as they are today because the technology did not yet exist, so carvings were made of the images, which were then printed onto the paper.

Photographs were often gruesome and not at all like the glorious war paintings of the past. Photographs of tired soldiers, filthy camps, war-torn towns, the sick, and the dead showed the reality of war. These images sent a message home that written reports could not.

Other sources of news included personal letters. Soldiers would write home about their experience at war and family would write back about life at home. Those at home drew information from these letters about where the army was located, the mood of the army, and the living situation of the soldiers. Soldiers enjoyed letters from home, which provided a break from life at war.

Left: Gen. Ambrose Burnside reads a newspaper. *Center:* A newspaper vendor near Union camp. *Right:* Morse code.

Pinpoint Where the *Hunley* Was Found

Description: The submarine H.L. *Hunley* made naval history when it sank an enemy warship in February, 1864. Named after its creator, Horace L. Hunley, the submarine was lost in battle, and its final location remained a mystery until long after the Civil War.

Built in Mobile, Alabama, and originally called the *Fish Boat,* it was shipped to Charleston, South Carolina, in 1863, but sank on a training exercise on August 29, killing its five crew members. The *Hunley* was raised and continued its training, but sank again on October 15, 1863, killing eight crew members this time, including Horace Hunley.

The submarine was raised a third time and on February 17, 1864, it attacked and sank the USS *Housatonic,* which was stationed five miles out to sea as part of a naval blockade of Charleston Harbor. Lieutenant George E. Dixon and his seven-man crew successfully embedded a barbed spar torpedo into the hull of the *Housatonic* and detonated it, sinking the ship and making naval history. But the *Hunley* failed to return to shore after the attack. No one was certain what happened or where the sub was located. The vessel and its men lay in a watery grave, missing for more than a century.

In 1970 the wreckage was located. Many organizations soon became involved in the attempt to raise the submarine, which had to be stabilized; it finally broke the surface of the ocean on the morning of August 8, 2000. The submarine has since been restored and can be visited at the Warren Lasch Conservation Center in Charleston.

Now you can also do a little investigative work of your own. Use Google Maps and the coordinates below to "drop a pin" in the exact location of the Hunley wreckage, or use a physical map and a pin.

N32° 43' 12" (or 32.72) / W79° 46' 30" (or -79.775)

The H.L. *Hunley,* the first submarine to sink an enemy ship.

 www.googlemaps.com

Find a Name from the Civil War

Description: The word search below contains the names of military leaders, participants, and soldiers from American history. Circle the names from the Civil War and draw a line through the names of those who served in other American engagements.

David Farragut

Braxton Bragg

Stonewall Jackson

George Washington

Philip Kearney

William Westmoreland

Chief Joseph

Loreta Janeta Velazquez

George G. Meade

William T. Sherman

John J. Pershing

Jeb Stuart

Jennie Hodgers

Dwight D. Eisenhower

James Longstreet

Edward Porter Alexander

Frederick Douglass

```
R  L  N  T  S  P  H  G  G  E  S  W  R  W  D
L  O  O  E  R  H  T  E  E  U  S  B  E  I  W
V  R  S  E  E  I  R  O  O  Y  A  A  D  L  I
T  E  K  R  G  L  S  R  R  S  L  K  N  L  G
T  T  C  T  D  I  N  G  G  D  G  Y  A  I  H
H  A  A  S  O  P  F  E  E  E  U  A  X  A  T
P  J  J  G  H  K  W  W  G  Y  O  V  E  M  D
E  A  L  N  E  E  C  A  M  V  D  Q  L  W  E
S  N  L  O  I  A  L  S  E  K  K  S  A  E  I
O  E  A  L  N  R  A  H  A  E  C  P  R  S  S
J  T  W  S  N  N  C  I  D  B  I  P  E  T  E
F  A  E  E  E  E  C  N  E  R  R  H  T  M  N
E  V  N  M  J  Y  I  G  Z  A  E  O  R  O  H
I  E  O  A  A  K  N  T  C  M  D  B  O  R  O
H  L  T  J  V  P  Z  O  C  H  E  P  P  E  W
C  A  S  Z  G  R  K  N  A  Z  R  E  D  L  E
X  Z  T  H  U  T  N  J  R  W  F  V  R  A  R
S  Q  J  E  B  S  T  U  A  R  T  D  A  N  E
G  U  O  J  M  S  I  X  S  T  M  D  W  D  I
D  E  Q  Y  E  W  X  X  F  G  L  J  D  W  I
G  Z  C  M  L  I  Y  Y  E  X  Z  S  E  O  D
N  A  M  R  E  H  S  T  M  A  I  L  L  I  W
D  A  V  I  D  F  A  R  R  A  G  U  T  Q  Z
G  N  I  H  S  R  E  P  J  N  H  O  J  H  U
B  R  A  X  T  O  N  B  R  A  G  G  J  B  O
```

Find the Animal Warriors

Description: Civil War soldiers often found comfort from the horrors of the battlefield in the company of a regimental or personal animal. Some followed their regiments or owners into battle, even sacrificing their lives for the cause. Match the animal warriors with their owners below, and then find their picture online—you'll be surprised by what you find.

A. Little Sorrell _____	1. This beloved mascot for the 11th Pennsylvania Volunteer Infantry "fought" with her regiment at Gettysburg and was killed at the battle of Hatcher's Run in Virginia.
B. Jack _____	2. This animal cost its owner $200 and would be a part of his owner's funeral procession. The general public came to adore him as much as his owner, pulling the hair from his tail for souvenirs.
C. Sallie _____	3. This mascot "fought" with the volunteer fireman of the 102nd Pennsylvania Infantry. He "fought" at the battles of the Wilderness, Spotsylvania, and Petersburg.
D. Traveller _____	4. This animal was present at the accidental shooting of his owner at Chancellorsville. He is currently on display at the Virginia Military Institute in Lexington, Virginia.
E. Douglas _____	5. Along with this animal, the 104th Ohio also had a Newfoundland dog, a cat, and a tamed raccoon as mascots.
F. Old Abe _____	6. One of the most unusual mascots in the Civil War, the 43rd Mississippi's mascot was killed at Vicksburg.
G. Old Harvey _____	7. This mascot "fought" in the battles of Corinth and the siege of Vicksburg with the 8th Wisconsin Company C. His image became the insignia of the US Army's 101st Airborne Division.
H. Rienzi _____	8. This animal was depicted on the coat of arms of the 69th New York wearing a green coat with "69" in gold letters. The 69th New York had two of them.
I. Irish Wolfhound _____	9. This animal's owner named him after a skirmish in Mississippi. After the animal's death in 1878, he was stuffed and donated to the Smithsonian for display.

Answers: 1:C, 2:D, 3:B, 4:A, 5:G, 6:E, 7:F, 8:I, 9:H

Be a History Detective

Description: Much of the study of history is detective work. Accurate historical information is sometimes difficult to find and must be dug up. Using and double-checking multiple sources in order to present a well-rounded perspective of the past are important components to historical study. Start your journey toward becoming a history detective here by completing this cryptogram. Here's a hint: The message is about someone you will read about in this book.

A	B	C	D	E	F	G	H	I	J	K	L	M	N	O	P	Q	R	S	T	U	V	W	X	Y	Z
		20		13		10					5		12				17	21	19						

```
 S  _  _       _  _  _   T    _  _   N  S    _  S  E  R    _  E      _  N    T    _  E
21 11 18      14 11 19  4  23 12 21  21 13 17 25 13  3   23 12   19  1 13

 _  R  S  T    T  E  N  N  E  S  S  E  E    _  N    _  N  T  R  _  ,
22 23 17 21 19 19 13 12 12 13 21 21 13 13  23 12   22 11 12 19 17  6

 C  _  _  _  _  _    N  .     _  E  S  R  _  _  _  E    _  T  _  E
20  8 18 15 11 12  6   1      1 13  21 24 17 25 23 25 13  3   19  1 13

 _  R  _  N    _  R  T  E  C    _  _  _  _  _  N    _  T  C  _  :
14 11 17  11 12  3   14 17  8 19 13  20  8 18 15 11 12  6   11  6 19 20  1

 R  _  ,    S    _  E  S  _  _    O    T    E    _  G    S
 8 17   11    21 23  3 13 21  1  8 14   8 22  19  1 13   7 23 10  21  1  8 14
```

Read/Watch

There are more than 80,000 books written about the American Civil War. In fact, there has been at least one book written for every day since the Civil War ended. But you don't need to read them all to learn about the war. In this section, you'll read some of the most significant books, letters, and speeches to get acquainted with the history and people involved in the war. Discover the war through the eyes of a young soldier, analyze a political cartoon, and memorize the Gettysburg Address.

In addition to reading about the war, there is also plenty to see. Ken Burns's Civil War documentary will capture the attention of almost anyone with his use of powerful images, music, and personal accounts. Witnessing a reenactment can spark the imagination and allow you to picture how a battle may have looked, sounded, or felt.

So find your comfy spot, prepare your snack, and get ready to learn more about the Civil War.

Decipher a Political Cartoon

Description: Political cartoons date back to the sixteenth century and were just as effective during the Civil War as they are today. Benjamin Franklin made use of a still-famous image captioned "Join or Die" to assist in gaining support for the American Revolution and Thomas Nast defended Abraham Lincoln's policies in *Frank Leslie's Weekly* during the Civil War. Deciphering a political cartoon can be tricky, since they most often mock the current events of the time. Read the following description of the cartoon and the events it references and see if you can decipher the cartoon by answering the questions that follow.

General Bombshells, the True Peace Candidate; or, the War Path the True One
Printed in *Frank Leslie's Budget of Fun* in November, 1864, "General Bombshells" makes reference to the 1864 Democratic National Convention in Chicago at which George B. McClellan became the nominee for the presidency. He proposed the Chicago Platform, a peace compromise with the Confederacy.

Wielding a sword that reads RIGHT MAKES MIGHT, General Bombshell, the animated cannon at the center of this cartoon, is seen breaking the table at which Confederate President Jefferson Davis stands, and from which hangs the Chicago Platform. McClellan's Reports have fallen to the ground and have been splattered with ink. John Bull, representing Great Britain, Peace Democrat Congressman Fernando Wood, and various members of the Northern press watch on in dismay. While pointing to himself, General Bombshell tells his audience, "Say Rebs! these are Uncle Sam's only authorized Negotiators—They know how to make PEACE," while the smoke from the cannonball flying through the air above his head reads, To ALL WHOM IT MAY CONCERN. Looking on from behind the animated cannon are, left to right, General Ulysses S. Grant, General William Tecumseh Sherman, and Admiral David Farragut. Approaching Union troops sing, "We are coming, Father Abram."

Make sure to use specific examples from the image to support your answers.

1. What important events are occurring at the time of the creation of this cartoon?

2. What does the title of the cartoon tell you?

3. What political statement do you think the artist is trying to make?

4. Are there biases or stereotypes? Can you tell what the artist's personal ideas are? What are they? How can you tell?

5. Who is the audience?

Experience the War through the Eyes of Sam Watkins

Description: Sam Watkins was twenty-one years old when he enlisted as a private in the First Tennessee Infantry in 1861. Assigned to Company H, he served the Confederate army throughout the entire war, fighting in more than twenty battles, including Shiloh, Chickamauga, Atlanta, and Franklin. Sam was one of only seven men from Company H left at the end of the war. Twenty years after the war, Sam's children and grandchildren encouraged him to write down his experiences so they would be able to pass his story along to their family. The result was *Company Aytch: Or, a Sideshow of the Big Show,* which was published in 1882. Today, his reflections are considered among the best accounts of a common soldier.

To gain a better understanding of the life of the common Civil War soldier, read the following excerpt from *Company Aytch:*

A soldier's life is not a pleasant one. It is always, at best, one of privations and hardships. The emotions of patriotism and pleasure hardly counterbalance the toil and suffering that he has to undergo in order to enjoy his patriotism and pleasure. Dying on the field of battle and glory is about the easiest duty a soldier has to undergo. It is the living, marching, fighting, shooting soldier that has the hardships of war to carry. When a brave soldier is killed he is at rest. The living soldier knows not at what moment he, too, may be called on to lay down his life on the altar of his country. The dead are heroes, the living are but men compelled to do the drudgery and suffer the privations incident to the thing called "glorious war." (109–110)

Impressions after the Battle of Chickamauga (September 19, 1863):

We remained upon the battlefield of Chickamauga all night. Everything had fallen into our hands. We had captured a great many prisoners and small arms, and many pieces of artillery and wagons and provisions. The Confederate and Federal dead, wounded, and dying were everywhere scattered over the battlefield. Men were lying where they fell, shot in every conceivable part of the body. . . . In fact, you might walk over the battlefield and find men shot from the crown of the head to the tip end of the toe. And then to see all those dead, wounded and dying horses. . . .

Reader, a battlefield, after the battle, is a sad and sorrowful sight to look at. The glory of war is but the glory of battle, the shouts, and cheers, and victory. (94)

Nicknames

Almost every soldier in the army—generals, colonels, captains, as well as privates—had a nick-name; and I almost believe that had the war continued ten years, we would have forgotten our proper names. John T. Tucker was called "Sneak," A.S. Horsley was called "Don Von One Horsley," W.A. Hughes was called "Apple Jack," Green Rieves was called "Old Snake," Bob Brank was called "Count," the colonel of the Fourth was called "Guide Post," E.L. Lansdown was called "Left Tenant," some were called by the name of "Greasy," some "Buzzard," others "Hog," and "Brutus," and "Cassius," and "Caesar," "Left Center," and "Bolderdust," and "Old Hannah"; in fact, the nick-names were singular and peculiar, and when a man got a nick-name it stuck to him like the Old Man of the Sea did to the shoulders of Sinbad, the sailor. (71)

A young Confederate private, roughly Sam's age.

Effects of the War

On April 9, 1865, Confederate General Robert E. Lee surrendered to United States General Ulysses S. Grant, essentially ending the Civil War.

The war had taken its toll, destroying cities, devastating the Southern economy, and claiming the lives of hundreds of thousands of Americans. After four long years, many just wanted to end the war as quickly and peacefully as possible.

Two years before the end of the war, President Lincoln proposed a plan for reunification that required states to get loyalty oaths from 10 percent of the population and to abolish slavery. Unfortunately, he would not put his plan in place, nor see the country reunified. On April 14, 1865, just five days after Lee's surrender, Lincoln was assassinated.

Now president, Andrew Johnson proposed a plan that was similar to Lincoln's in that it did not require a great deal from former Confederate states to reenter the Union. Not everyone agreed with his proposal and in 1867, after much back and forth between Johnson and Congress, Congress passed the Reconstruction Act. Under this act, states were required to disband their former governments, write new constitutions, ratify the Fourteenth Amendment, and allow black men to vote.

While dealing with the issue of Reconstruction, the federal government was also busy working on some major changes to the US Constitution—the Thirteenth, Fourteenth, and Fifteenth Amendments. In 1865, the Thirteenth Amendment, the first addition since the war, was ratified, abolishing slavery in the United States. In 1868, the Fourteenth Amendment was ratified, defining citizenship and preventing states from interfering with the rights of citizens as defined in the Constitution. In 1870, the Fifteenth Amendment was ratified, extending the right to vote to black men.

Immediately after the war, major strides were made to reunify the country and provide equality for African Americans. However, these were only the first steps. Reunification, recovery, and racial equality continued to be issues for many years and, to some extent, continue to this day.

Reconstruction: The period following the Civil War in which Congress passed laws designed to rebuild the country and bring the Southern states back into the Union.
Amendment: An addition or change.
Ratify: To give approval or agree to something.

THE ASSASSINATION OF PRESIDENT LINCOLN.
AT FORD'S THEATRE WASHINGTON, D.C. APRIL 14TH 1865.

Top: An African-American family poses in front of the ruins of Richmond in April 1865. *Bottom:* A Currier & Ives lithograph of the assassination of President Lincoln.

Experience a Reenactment

Description: Have you ever wondered what a real Civil War battlefield looked like, sounded like, or smelled like, packed with thousands of soldiers, artillery, and horses? A good reenactment can help you imagine, as you experience the boom of the cannons, the haze of the smoke, and the confusion of a battle. Of course, no cannonballs are flying, no bullets are whizzing through the air, and no one is getting killed, but it nevertheless provides a real glimpse at what a Civil War battle or encampment might have looked like. These events simply have to be experienced at least once. Check online for locations and times of these events.

150th anniversary reenactment of the Battle of Bull Run.

Memorize the Gettysburg Address

Description: On November 19, 1863, in Gettysburg, Pennsylvania, Abraham Lincoln asked that "the brave men, living and dead, who struggled" as soldiers in the Civil War not be forgotten. Most importantly, Lincoln asked the American people to remember the noble reasons for the fight. Today, his speech is among the most famous in American history, despite his humble line, "the world will little note nor long remember what we say here." Memorize this unforgettable speech and recite it for your friends and family members.

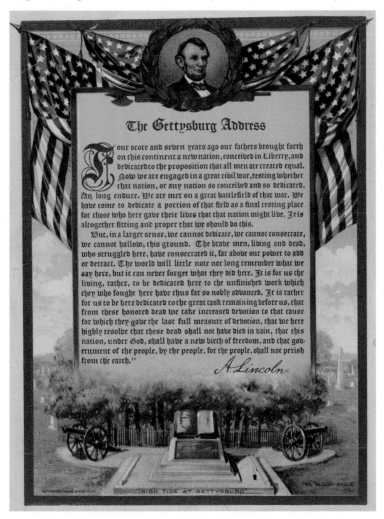

Read *Eyewitness: Civil War*

Description: Learn how to fire a cannon, what soldiers carried into battle, and about the tools of a Civil War surgeon in John Stanchak's book, *Eyewitness: Civil War.* Meet Southern Spy Belle Boyd, slave hero Robert Smalls, and legendary commanders like Robert E. Lee and Ulysses S. Grant. Explore the adventure and lore of America's greatest conflict with dramatic pictures of the Confederate capital in ruins, propaganda posters, and photographs of fighting men and the people they left behind.

Read the Johnny Clem Poem

Description: Sometimes it is difficult to tell what is factual and what has been created for dramatic effect. When a movie or a TV show is "based on actual events," this may not always mean that it is historically accurate. The same was true during and after the Civil War. In the years following the Civil War many books, songs, plays, and poems were written that could not be verified as fact, but which served to stir the hearts of Americans. That is the case for a poem written by William S. Hays for *Harpers Weekly* magazine called "The Drummer Boy of Shiloh." While the poem, also a song, was popular in its day, historians think that Hays's "Drummer Boy of Shiloh" most closely resembles the factual story of Johnny Clem—the drummer boy of Chickamauga.

Johnny's story is dramatic in its own right. At the age of ten, Johnny ran away from his Ohio home and attempted to enlist with the 3rd Ohio infantry. He was turned away, but was soon adopted as drummer boy and mascot by the 22nd Michigan. He had originally been refused by the 22nd but found a home there when he tagged along despite their refusal to muster him in. It is unlikely that Johnny participated in the Battle of Shiloh. However, it is probable that Johnny Clem did participate in the Battle of Chickamauga, where he shot a Confederate colonel who demanded his surrender. He was promoted to sergeant and became the youngest noncommissioned officer in the US Army.

Regardless of its authenticity, Hays's poem tells the story of a young drummer boy who dies in battle. His comrades kneel around him weeping and listen to the boy's prayers as he dies. The poem reflects upon the great number of soldiers, like the drummer boy, who "pray[ed] before they died." The poem is as poignant today as it was then and is well worth reading.

Union drummer boy John Clem at Point Lookout, Tennessee.

The Drummer Boy of Shiloh

"Look down upon the battlefield,
Oh Thou, Our Heavenly Friend,
Have mercy on our sinful souls."
The soldiers cried, "Amen."
There gathered 'round a little group,
Each brave man knelt and cried
They listened to the drummer boy,
Who prayed before he died.

"Oh, Mother," said the dying boy,
"Look down from heaven on me.
Receive me to thy fond embrace,
Oh, take me home to thee.
I've loved my country as my God.
To serve them both I've tried."
He smiled, shook hands —death seized the boy,
Who prayed before he died.

Each soldier wept then like a child.
Stout hearts were they and brave.
They wrapped him in his country's flag
And laid him in the grave.
They placed by him the Bible,
A rededicated guide
To those that mourn the drummer boy
Who prayed before he died.

Ye angels 'round the throne of grace,
Look down upon the braves,
Who fought and died on Shiloh's plain,
Now slumbering in their graves.
How many homes made desolate,
How many hearts have sighed.
How many like that drummer boy,
Who prayed before he died.

—William S. Hays

Watch Ken Burns's Miniseries, *The Civil War*

Description: Ken Burns's *The Civil War* first aired on PBS in 1990. Providing a narrated timeline of the war along with personal accounts, it makes you aware of what life was like for people at that time. With forty million viewers, it was the most watched program ever shown on PBS and is still a favorite documentary for many.

You might like to enjoy a snack while you watch the movie. Consider concocting a snack mix containing food items from the time of the Civil War. Popcorn, pretzels, and peanuts were popular items at the time. Americans had learned how to make popcorn from the Native Americans upon their arrival in the seventeenth century and pretzels were brought to America by German and Swiss immigrants who settled largely in Pennsylvania and became known as the "Pennsylvania Dutch." Peanuts were known as "goober peas" and were popular among Confederate soldiers as an emergency ration. A popular song called "Goober Peas" was sung among Confederate soldiers—you can check it out on YouTube or Wikipedia.

It is thought that jelly beans were invented in 1861 by Boston confectioner William Schraff, who urged people to send his jelly beans to soldiers. Jelly beans didn't see nationwide popularity until the turn of the century, but if your snack requires a little something more, feel free to add this sweet treat to your mix.

Preservation

Why did battles take place in certain spots? Did armies walk around the countryside until they saw one another and then start fighting?

While sometimes skirmishes were simply a matter of finding the enemy along the way, battles usually occurred when one side was defending something of importance or trying to obtain something of importance such as a railroad junction, fort, or city. Battles were also fought in certain geographic locations because there were strategic advantages such as high ground or natural barriers.

5 Reasons Why Battles Happen in Certain Places

Railroad and road networks: Important for the transportation of troops and supplies.

Waterways: Control of certain waterways prevents the enemy from moving beyond that waterway. Waterways also allow for transportation of troops and supplies.

Importance of the location: Capturing the capital of the enemy will almost certainly end the war. The Army of Northern Virginia and The Army of the Potomac were constantly trying to move around one another to capture the opposing army's capital. Both armies had to be on the offense and defense.

Topography: Geographically a certain location will offer more useful features for a battle such as a river, hills, natural barriers, or preexisting covering.

Intelligence: Reliable information on the location of the enemy was rare and could lead to a battle.

Civil War battlefields are the best place to learn about the history of the war. They give you the opportunity to walk where the soldiers walked, to see what they saw, and to understand their fear, excitement, and courage. There is no better way to understand the Confederate position at the Battle of Fredericksburg than to actually stand behind the stone wall there. There is no better way to realize the violent fighting at the Battle of Franklin than to visit the bullet-riddled Carter House.

Battlefields, while focusing on the specific battle, also present the bigger picture. By learning about the timing and location of a battle, you can understand what was going on militarily, politically, and socially at that point in the war. By visiting Bull Run, the first battle of the war, you can learn why the battle was fought at that particular spot, how civilians and soldiers felt about the battle, and what happened politically because of this battle.

Now that you are familiar with all the ways to study history and have a great understanding of the American Civil War, this is your opportunity to get involved. Become part of the historic preservation efforts that started after the Battle of Gettysburg. You can protect the history of the war and provide awesome history lessons for generations to come. Get involved by visiting the Civil War Trust's website at www.civilwar.org.

Antietam Battlefield

Study the Letters of Former Slave, Private Samuel Cabble

Description: Black troops served in support positions from the beginning of the war, but the creation of the United States Colored Troops (USCT) allowed for African Americans to serve as combat troops. By war's end, 180,000 black men wore Federal uniforms. Samuel Cabble, a twenty-one-year-old private in the 54th Massachusetts Infantry (colored), was a slave before he joined the army. At the end of the war he returned home to his wife in Missouri and together they moved to Denver, Colorado.

Dear Wife i have enlisted in the army i am now in the state of Massachusetts but before this letter reaches you i will be in North Carlinia and though great is the present national dificulties yet i look forward to a brighter day When i shall have the opertunity of seeing you in the full enjoyment of fredom i would like to no if you are still in slavery if you are it will not be long before we shall have crushed the system that now opreses you for in the course of three months you shall have your liberty. great is the outpouring of the colered peopl that is now rallying with the hearts of lions against that very curse that has seperated you an me yet we shall meet again and oh what a happy time that will be when this ungodly rebellion shall be put down and the curses of our land is trampled under our feet i am a soldier now and i shall use my utmost endeavor to strike at the rebellion and the heart of this system that so long has kept us in chains . . . remain your own afectionate husband until death—Samuel Cabble

An African-American man sits outside a military camp tent.

View a Civil War Photo in 3-D

Description: Did you know that about 70 percent of all Civil War battlefield photographs were shot as "stereoviews," the nineteenth-century equivalent of 3-D? To create a stereoview image, photographers used a twin-lens camera to capture the same image from two separate lenses, in much the same way that two human eyes capture the same image from slightly different angles on the head. Once processed, the photographer would place the two stereo images onto a viewing card—the stereograph or stereoview card. These stereoview cards could then be easily inserted into widely available viewers creating a 3-D image. See for yourself! Go to www.civilwar.org/3D to get a free pair of 3-D glasses and to see some amazing Civil War 3-D images.

Put on your 3D glasses to see how this photograph was *meant* to be seen.

PRESERVE

The Civil War Trust is the only national nonprofit organization dedicated to preserving America's hallowed Civil War battlegrounds.

EDUCATE

The Civil War Trust is committed to educating the public about America's Civil War heritage, through interpretive walking trails and teacher programs.

ENJOY

The Civil War Trust works with government officials and other nonprofits to encourage tourists to visit and enjoy preserved Civil War battlefields.

To learn more about the Civil War and to help the Civil War Trust in its mission, visit:

CIVILWAR.ORG